KILLER ANIMALS
LIONS
ON THE HUNT

by Lori Polydoros

Reading Consultant:
Barbara J. Fox
Reading Specialist
North Carolina State University

Content Consultant:
Micaela Szykman Gunther, PhD
Assistant Professor, Department of Wildlife
Humboldt State University
Arcata, California

Capstone

Mankato, Minnesota

Blazers is published by Capstone Press,
151 Good Counsel Drive, P.O. Box 669, Mankato, Minnesota 56002.
www.capstonepress.com

Library of Congress Cataloging-in-Publication Data
Polydoros, Lori, 1968–
    Lions: on the hunt/by Lori Polydoros.
    p. cm. — (Blazers. Killer animals)
    Includes bibliographical references and index.
    Summary: "Describes lions, their physical features, how they hunt and kill, and their role in the ecosystem" — Provided by publisher.
    ISBN-13: 978-1-4296-2319-3 (hardcover)
    ISBN-10: 1-4296-2319-5 (hardcover)
    1. Lions — Juvenile literature. I. Title.
QL737.C23P65 2009
599.757 — dc22
                    2008029837

Editorial Credits
Abby Czeskleba, editor; Kyle Grenz, designer; Wanda Winch, photo researcher

Photo Credits
Art Life Images/Winfried Wisniewski, 6–7
Corbis/Royalty-Free, 26–27
Creatas, cover
Getty Images Inc./Minden Pictures/Mitsuaki Iwago, 12–13; Pete Oxford, 18–19, 28–29;
    National Geographic/Beverly Joubert, 10–11; Riser/Paul Souders, 8; The Image Bank/Art
    Wolfe, 4–5; Joseph Van Os, 22–23
iStockphoto/Wolfgang Steiner, 17
Minden Pictures/Martin Harvey, 24
Peter Arnold/C & M Denis-Huot, 20–21
Shutterstock/Christian Musat, 14–15

1 2 3 4 5 6   14 13 12 11 10 09

TABLE OF CONTENTS

ON THE ATTACK

A **lioness** hides in the grass near a herd of wildebeest. She creeps toward an old bull.

lioness – a female lion

The chase is on! The lioness rushes toward the bull. She drives him into the jaws of two other lionesses. They bring the wildebeest down. Dinner for the **pride** is served.

pride – a group of lions that live together

PAWS AND
CLAWS

Lions are some of the largest wild cats in the world. Male lions weigh up to 500 pounds (227 kilograms). They are about 8 feet (2.4 meters) long. Lionesses weigh up to 300 pounds (136 kilograms). They are 6 feet (1.8 meters) long.

Killer Fact

Tigers are the only wild cats that are bigger than lions.

Lionesses do most of the hunting for the pride. **Prey** can be twice the size of a lioness. Lionesses may leap more than 30 feet (9 meters) to pounce on prey.

prey – an animal hunted by another animal for food

Lions have strong jaws and sharp teeth to tear meat. They swallow their food in big chunks. Deadly claws and teeth make them fierce hunters.

Lions use their strong senses for hunting. They can see five times better than humans. Lions can hear their prey more than 1 mile (1.6 kilometers) away. Lions use their sense of smell to find food.

15

HUNTING MACHINES

Lionesses carefully **stalk** their prey. They hide behind tall grass or brush until they attack. Lionesses may hunt alone or in groups.

stalk – to hunt an animal in a quiet, secret way

KILLER FACT

Lions can run more than 30 miles
(48 kilometers) per hour.

A lioness runs toward prey at a lightning-fast speed. She leaps onto prey and knocks it down.

KILLER FACT

Male lions eat first. The cubs eat last.

A lioness kills prey by biting its throat. She may also bite the **muzzle** or the back of its neck. She keeps biting until the animal stops breathing.

muzzle – an animal's nose, mouth, and jaws

long tail

strong leg

round ear

furry mane

front paw

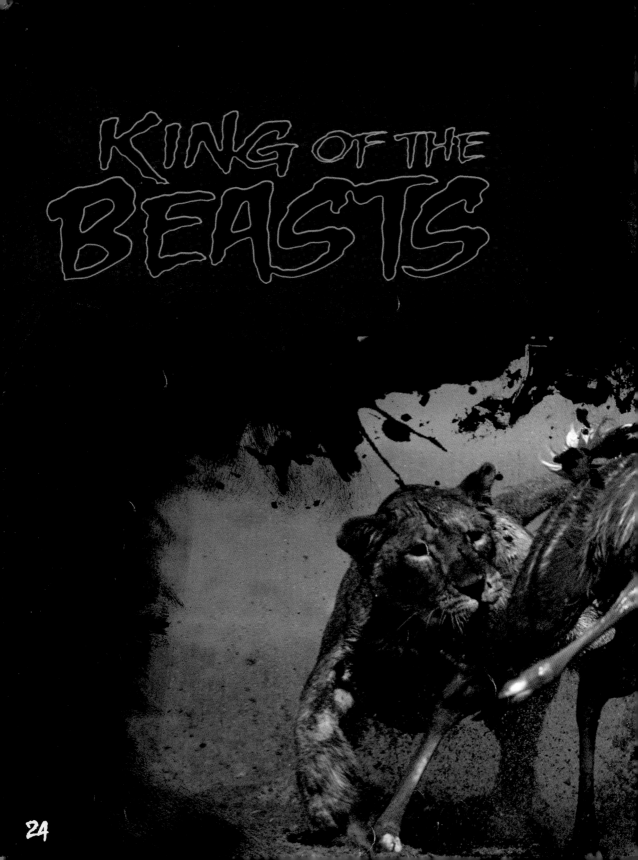

KING OF THE
BEASTS

Lions help balance the number of animals in the **ecosystem**. They eat zebras, wildebeest, and antelope. Without lions, there would be too many animals and not enough food.

ecosystem – a group of animals and plants that work together with their surroundings

Lions are fierce animals, but they rarely attack people. Sadly, people kill lions for their skin and claws. People must protect the king of the beasts so they can **survive**.

survive – to continue to live

Ready to Pounce!

GLOSSARY

ecosystem (EE-koh-sis-tuhm) — a group of animals and plants that work together with their surroundings

herd (HURD) — a large group of animals that lives or moves together

lioness (LYE-uh-ness) — a female lion

muzzle (MUHZ-uhl) — an animal's nose, mouth, and jaws

pounce (POUNSS) — to jump on something suddenly and grab it

prey (PRAY) — an animal hunted by another animal for food

pride (PRIDE) — a group of lions that live together

stalk (STAWK) — to hunt an animal in a quiet, secret way

survive (sur-VIVE) — to continue to live

Read More

Joubert, Beverly, and Dereck Joubert. *Face to Face with Lions*. Washington, D.C.: National Geographic, 2008.

Rau, Dana Meachen. *The Lion in the Grass*. Benchmark Rebus. New York: Marshall Cavendish Benchmark, 2007.

Thomas, Isabel. *Lion vs. Tiger*. Animals Head to Head. Chicago: Raintree, 2006.

Internet Sites

FactHound offers a safe, fun way to find educator-approved Internet sites related to this book.

Here's what you do:

1. Visit *www.facthound.com*
2. Choose your grade level.
3. Begin your search.

This book's ID number is 9781429623193.

FactHound will fetch the best sites for you!

INDEX